THE
JOY
OF *Believing*

ARDETH G. KAPP

DESERET
BOOK

SALT LAKE CITY, UTAH

Interior images courtesy of picturesnow.com

Visit us at DeseretBook.com

Library of Congress Cataloging-in-Publication Data

Kapp, Ardeth Greene, 1931-
  The joy of believing / Ardeth G. Kapp.
    p. cm.
  ISBN 978-1-59038-809-9 (hardback : alk. paper)
  1. Christmas. 2. Christian life—Mormon authors. I. Title.
  BV45.K365 2007
  263'.915—dc22   2007021171

Printed in the United States of America
Worzalla Publishing Co., Stevens Point, WI

10   9   8   7   6   5   4   3   2   1

CONTENTS

1

"DO YOU BELIEVE IN SANTA?"

It wasn't even close to Christmas. It was summertime, around the middle of August, in Phoenix, Arizona. The temperature was hot. However, that didn't interfere in any way with the outdoor interests of four enthusiastic young brothers. Their backyard was filled with an invitation to a variety of activities to consume their thoughts and interest. There was the fire pit at one end of the wide, circular cement path that surrounded the lawn. At the other end was the basketball hoop that had consumed their attention for some time as they cheered for each other every time the ball managed to go through the hoop.

Sitting on the low brick wall surrounding the fire pit, I watched the boys as they moved from one activity to another. After two or three trips along the cement path, each time

1

increasing the speed on his skateboard, seven-year-old Josh let go with one hand and waved, with a smile that celebrated his grand performance. It seemed he was totally consumed with the acquired skill he was demonstrating to an appreciative audience of one. One more trip around the circle and he came full speed toward me. His eyes bright, and in a most serious tone, he posed a question: "Nana Ardie," he asked, "do you believe in Santa?" I had no idea what prompted his question. But Josh's curious and inquiring mind often caught me off guard.

"Do you believe in Santa?" is a question that invites thoughtful consideration before giving an honest answer to a trusting child. I asked myself, "*Do* you believe in Santa?" Into my mind came a review of the many lessons Josh and his brothers had been given by his parents, grandparents, teachers, and loved ones about the importance of honesty, integrity, and trust. I sensed from the tone of his voice and the look in his eye that this was not the first time he had pondered the question, "Is there a Santa?" Why it surfaced in the middle of the summer while riding a skateboard at top speed I did not understand. But now was the time he needed an answer.

I searched for an appropriate response.

"Let me answer your question, Josh, so you will never outgrow your love for Santa and all that he stands for." I motioned for him to sit beside me on the wall by the fire pit where we would be roasting wieners and marshmallows at sundown. He seemed intent on what I might have to say.

Looking into his trusting eyes, I began. "Let me tell you what I know about Santa, and then I'll ask you the question—is that okay?"

"Sure," he said.

"But first we'll talk about some other things that are also very important. Is that okay?"

"Sure."

A tall pole in a neighbor's backyard was the perfect place to begin. "Josh," I said, pointing in that direction, "what do you see hanging from that pole?"

"The flag," he quickly answered.

"Is it really a flag or just a big piece of cloth?"

"No," he insisted. "It's the flag of the United States of America."

"How do you know it's a flag? Tell me about it."

He was eager to explain. "It's red and white and blue and has stars and stripes on it."

"Is it important?"

"Yeah," he responded with conviction.

"It's important to me, too, Josh. You see, it serves as a symbol

3

so that we will always remember and never forget the blessing and the price paid for our freedom in this great land of America. Some people who don't believe in what the flag stands for want to burn it. We know what it stands for, and we want to honor it and be true to the responsibility of being good citizens. We often repeat the words 'I pledge allegiance to the flag of the United States of America, and to the republic for which it stands. . . . ' We know the flag stands for something very important. When you see the flag, does it ever look like just a big piece of cloth?"

"No," he insisted, "it is a flag. Sometimes I put my hand over my heart when it goes by me."

"How does it make you feel?"

"Good."

"Me, too."

"Symbols like the flag are very precious to us. Would you like to learn about another important symbol?"

"Yeah."

"Do you remember the big eagle that Papa Heber has on his desk in the library where we go to read all those fun books, and that large painting of the eagle in your brother's bedroom? What do you know about an eagle that is important?"

Josh looked a bit puzzled. What did this have to do with his initial question?

4

"Josh," I explained, "one day you will follow your brothers and become an Eagle Scout. An Eagle Scout is a boy who has reached the highest level in many important areas in Scouting. The reason he is called an Eagle Scout is that the eagle has been honored from the beginning of time. The eagle serves as a symbol or a reminder of something very important, a great accomplishment. The eagle is on the flags of many nations. The eagle spreads its mighty wings and soars high in the sky, even in a storm. The eagle stands for freedom and is the symbol of our great nation.

"Now I have a question for you, Josh. Do you believe in the flag?"

"Yes."

"Is it real?"

"Yes, it is."

"Do you believe in the eagle?"

Again his response was quick and sure. "Yes."

"Me, too, Josh. Can you see how symbols are very precious to us? They can affect how we feel, how we believe, and even how we behave. They help us remember.

"Now let's talk about Santa Claus. How does thinking about Santa make you feel?"

"Happy, 'cause it's about Christmas."

"That's right. And when we think of Christmas, Santa is a

5

very important part of that great celebration. It is a time when we think of giving gifts and receiving gifts. We can go to the shopping mall, and maybe we won't see a flag or an eagle but we might see Santa. And then we would be reminded of the love he has for everyone. When we see a kind, happy, rather fat man in a bright red suit, trimmed in white, and a beard and a big 'ho! ho!' laugh, we know it is Christmastime. We sometimes think of Santa at the North Pole, but Santa is also at the South Pole. He is in England and America. At Christmastime he is everywhere where people, and especially families, come together to share gifts of love and appreciation."

This seven-year-old boy with an inquisitive mind had been very patient as we shared our thoughts and feelings. Now, before I asked him to answer his own question, I wanted to let him know my honest feelings. "Josh," I explained, looking into his innocent bright eyes, "all my life I have believed in Santa, and all Santa stands for. He helps us want to love and serve everyone and be especially happy at Christmastime. I believe in the flag and all the good our flag stands for. I believe the eagle is real, and when you are an Eagle Scout you will learn more about the eagle. Now I'd like to ask you the question you asked me: Josh, do you believe in Santa?"

Josh nodded his head with a knowing smile.

"Me, too," I said.

A warm hug even on a hot summer day is like a period at the end of an important discussion. Oh, the joy of believing! Josh happily returned to his skateboard, wiser than he was before.

 2

"IS IT OKAY TO BELIEVE JUST ONE MORE YEAR?"

A few years ago, my little niece approached her mother one December day as the spirit of Christmas began awakening. The gift-giving symbolized by Santa Claus and the other wonderful traditions were emerging with each new day. In a quiet moment away from the hustle and bustle, this little girl, with her heart full of childlike excitement and yet on the verge of growing up, cornered her mother and, in all soberness, posed this thoughtful question: "Mom, is it okay if I believe just one more year?"

In our grown-up world, sometimes we quit asking the questions because we are sure we already know the answers. And yet with each new year, there awakens within our hearts a yearning to reach far enough to somehow comprehend more fully the significance of that singular event, the birth of the Savior of the world and what it means to each one of us individually and col-lectively, as brothers and sisters, disciples, Latter-day Saints. Off in a quiet corner, we might well ask ourselves, "What think ye of Christ?"

An unknown author made this observation:

> *Though Christ a thousand times in*
> *Bethlehem be born*
> *If He is not born in thee, thy soul is*
> *still forlorn.*

And even though we know the answer, consider with me this question: Is it okay if I believe just one more year? Yes, there is joy in believing in Santa Claus—but how much more in believing in Jesus Christ.

In celebrating the event of the birth of our Savior, there are many pageants, plays, programs, and performances. Having taught elementary school for a number of years, I can personally give account of a varied number of Josephs and Marys, old bathrobes tucked up and tied around little bodies to give some resemblance to shepherds, and "angels" with tinsel halos made from coat hang-ers mounted in such a way as to keep the halos attached to the heads of the constantly moving little angels. You could always tell the wise men from the shepherds because they carried oddly shaped boxes adorned with jewels brought from home. Faithful parents would come: fathers in business suits looking as if they may have just slipped out from some large business meeting and mothers and grandmothers sitting on little chairs far too small for comfort.

As a teacher, I would take my place midway between the performers and the audience. I never did quite determine where the greater performance was taking place. Was it on the makeshift stage or in the audience, where each pair of radiant eyes was riveted on performers as though each one were doing a solo number?

Perhaps you are familiar with the story of the school pageant where the little innkeeper forgot his lines and responded from his heart instead. When Joseph asked if there was room in the inn, the young innkeeper hesitated and the prompter whispered his lines from the wings: "There is no room. Be gone." The young innkeeper repeated the words. The young actor playing Joseph sadly placed his arm around Mary, and, according to the script and the rehearsal, the two little people who had rehearsed their lines so well started to move away. Suddenly this Christmas pageant became different from any other. "Don't go, Joseph!" the innkeeper cried out. "Bring Mary back. She can have *my* room."

Contrary to the historical account of this event, in this pageant there was room in the inn. The room was in the innkeeper's own room; it was in his heart. The question we each must ask ourselves in our overcrowded lives is this: Is there room in our inns? Will we take the Savior into our lives, into our hearts, into our very souls, so that He becomes the center of our lives?

Late one evening the Christmas lights sparkled like jewels as my husband and I drove through the snow-packed streets to the outskirts of town. The lights were not as plentiful there, but each colorful bulb added beauty to the more humble homes nestled together in the gently falling snow. Driving down one street and then another, we tried with difficulty to read the street signs. Finally we found the address we were looking for. Making our way through the deep snow of the unshoveled walk, we rang the doorbell and were immediately greeted by Brent, an eight-year-old boy. He invited us in. The living room was small but was made warm and cozy by a fire burning in the fireplace. The boy's eighty-six-year-old grandfather, with his leg in a cast, rested on the couch near the Christmas tree. He had slipped off the roof while attempting to shovel the heavy snow that had fallen the night before.

As we exchanged greetings and hugs, Brent stood anxiously waiting for the first opportunity to ask a question. In a most forthright and direct way he asked, "Have you ever shaken hands with the prophet?" The eagerness with which he asked gave me reason to believe that he may have rehearsed that question in his mind several times in anticipation of our visit.

"Yes, Brent," I said, "I have shaken the hand of the prophet."

"Oh," he said. His eyes were wide, and his voice reminded me of what a great privilege that is. "If only I could just shake the hand of the prophet." His tone suggested that such an experience would surely be the greatest Christmas gift he could receive. And if not the greatest, at least it would be among the very best.

Sensing the love and respect Brent obviously felt for our prophet, and wanting to somehow provide a tie between the prophet and the young boy, I reached out my hand. "Brent," I said, "this hand has shaken the hand of the prophet."

He grabbed my hand and shook it vigorously. Then he let go and turned his hand over from front to back to examine it thoroughly. "I'll never wash my hand," he said. Considering the problems this decision might cause, I suggested that he probably should wash his hand and just keep the memory in his mind. This suggestion was not acceptable. He had a better idea. "Okay," he said. "I'll wash my hand, but I'll save the water." That seemed like a good suggestion, although I supposed he was only joking.

Brent left the room. A few minutes later, he returned, this time carrying a plastic bag dripping with water. Before anyone could question him, he proudly announced, "I washed my hand,"

and held up the bag full of water for all to see. We talked about the water in the bag and how that was a distant connection to the prophet. Then our visit about Christmases past continued. Brent sat on the floor facing the Christmas tree, his knees peeking through his faded blue jeans, and from the corner of my eye I watched him examine the bag of water as if he were expecting to see some evidence that this was holy water. The fire burned low, and the lights on the tree seemed to brighten.

After a few minutes, Brent got up and, taking his treasure with him, left the room. While I wondered if we would see him again before we left, he returned, this time without the plastic bag. He had determined a better solution for his desire to be in touch with the prophet. Standing in the doorway with his T-shirt wet all the way down the front, he explained what he had done. "I drank the water," he said.

This creative solution was not to be viewed as a joke or something to be made fun of. Brent was serious. He was carrying something important, not on the outside where he could lay it down, but on the inside. The water from the hand that he had washed, a hand that had shaken the hand of someone who had shaken the hand of the prophet, was now part of him, on the inside, and he would keep it. He made room on the inside.

Would this really make any difference? What did it really

mean to Brent? It was much more than water, I was sure. But in the rush of the Christmas season, the incident slipped from my mind until a few days later. Then at sacrament meeting on the Sunday before Christmas, I received some understanding of what this young boy was feeling and wanting. The Sunday before Christmas brings a sensitivity that makes important things even more important, a time of recommitment and rededication, of sorrow for wrongdoings and of resolve and hope to do better in the new year. The sacramental prayer had been offered, and the sacred emblems were being passed quietly and reverently. As the sister on my right passed the sacrament tray to me and held it while I raised the small cup of water to my lips, into my mind came this thought: "I want to get this water on the inside."

I thought of Brent, a newly baptized member. I remembered the baptismal covenant. I thought of the symbolism of the water, the washing away of our sins. The cup of water of which I would partake renewed the promises and blessings of the atonement of Jesus Christ. It was His birth we were celebrating. I could hear in my mind again the sacramental prayer on the water: " . . . that they do always remember him, that they may have his Spirit to be with them." The water symbolizes His blood, which was shed for each of us so that we might live and have eternal life. "Thank you, Brent," I said to myself, "for this wonderful gift you have given me: an increased desire to drink the water, the symbol of His atonement, to get it on the inside, to make room in my life for Him so that I might become more like Him."

To the question from Brent, "Have you ever shaken hands with the prophet?" my answer is yes. But I have also shaken hands with a little eight-year-old boy, and I've learned important and eternal truths from both.

President Marion G. Romney gave us great insight when he explained: "Now there is a doctrine abroad in the world today which teaches that the physical emblems of the sacrament are transformed into the flesh and blood of Jesus. We do not teach such a doctrine, for we know that any transformation which comes from the administration of the sacrament takes place in the souls of those who understandingly partake of it. It is the participating individuals who are affected, and they are affected in a most marvelous way, for they are given the Spirit of the Lord to be with them" (in Conference Report, April 1946, 40).

In the spring of 1980, my husband and I went up from Galilee, out of the city of Nazareth, into Judea, unto the town of Bethlehem. We walked the paths where Jesus walked and felt His presence there. We stood outside of Jerusalem beneath the gnarled olive trees in the Garden of Gethsemane, where the Savior of the world suffered and shed drops of blood.

As we looked on the brow of the hill at Golgotha, we could hear in our minds the words, "Father, forgive them, for they know not what they do." We envisioned the setting of the Last Supper, where He may have been thinking of the imminent events that were to follow and where He taught His apostles and gave the commandment to love one another. We thought of Him moving up the streets of the old city, carrying the cross toward Golgotha, because there was no room for Him in the hearts of the persecutors. In the quiet of that hour, we each asked ourselves, "Why did He do this all for me? How in God's name can I ever repay Him?" And we wondered if we, like the innkeeper, would call, "Come back, come back. You can have my room. My heart. My time. My life. My vote. I give it all. All that I have. All that I am. All that I ever hope to be."

Oh, yes, it is okay to believe *in Christ* one more year and another and another and another. We believe in God, the Eternal Father, and in His Son, Jesus Christ, and in the Holy Ghost. We believe that through the atonement of Christ, all mankind may be saved through obedience to the laws and ordinances of the gospel. At those times when we feel least worthy, least comfortable about carrying His holy name, and have a keener sense of our imperfections—those moments when the flesh is weak and our spirits suffer disappointments, knowing what we *can* become—we

17

might feel a sense of withdrawing, a pulling away, a feeling of needing to set aside, for a time at least, that divine relationship with the Savior until we are more worthy. It is at that very moment, even in our unworthiness, that the offer is again given to us to accept the great gift of the atonement, even before we change. When we feel the need to pull away, we can reach out to Him. Instead of feeling the need to resist, we can submit to His will and partake of His gifts. What do we give in return? Love to one another. Then, as our faith grows stronger, His Spirit fills our hearts. The Light of Christ burns brightly, and we take upon us His countenance.

3

"ALL HEARTS RETURN HOME FOR CHRISTMAS"

Christmas growing up in Alberta, Canada, was always white and always cold. But besides the cold temperatures, I remember the deep feeling of warmth, that happy feeling of being together as our parents, four aunts, uncles, and many cousins of all ages gathered at our grandparents' big three-story house, where we remained from Christmas Eve all the way through New Year's Day.

This tradition must have seemed strange to the folks in our small town of Glenwood, since all of our aunts and uncles and cousins lived only a few blocks away from each other —within walking distance—all year long. It was not inconvenient for our dads and brothers to return home night and morning to milk the cows, do the chores, and be back in time for our large and happy family breakfast and evening supper. During the morning we played games and listened to favorite stories told and retold by our grandmother as we gathered around the large grate in the floor that let the heat pour out from the furnace below. In the afternoon we practiced for the evening's talent show while our mothers made pies and cakes. I don't remember what our dads did during the day, but they joined us as we all gathered for supper. And after the evening meal we presented a talent show to a very responsive audience, who all sang together. We had a family orchestra, and it was agreed, especially by our grandpa, that we were a very musical family.

One of the family secrets we kept and seldom discussed except at Christmastime was the unusual accommodations that were available for the older boys in the family. In the attic of Grandpa and Grandma Leavitt's house, the elders quorum had arranged to store the long wooden boxes they had made for coffins. These would be used as the need arose, at which time the Relief Society would finish the inside of the box with padding and with beautiful white satin. Sleeping in the box-like coffins was a ritual our brothers quite enjoyed—until one year when Uncle Ted, unbeknown to the boys, took a resting place in one of the boxes in the corner of the upstairs attic. Of course, light sleeping the night before Christmas was to be expected—the slightest sound would awaken you to the possibility that Christmas morning had finally arrived. This particular Christmas Eve, around midnight, Uncle Ted made a sound, then raised up from his sleeping position covered with a white sheet. Christmas morning came very early that year, at least for the boys in the attic.

Our Christmas morning tradition required everyone to wait at the top of the stairs until we could all go down together and gather around the big Christmas tree in the parlor. We had decorated our tree with strings of popcorn and cranberries. At the bottom of the stairs we waited for what seemed an awfully long time while Grandpa gave the family prayer. I remember wondering if the reason he prayed for so long was that, all together, we made such a big family. It seemed to me that each year, as our family grew bigger, his prayers got longer.

After the presents were opened and the wrappings were put away, we, as many as could fit, climbed on the sleigh with big runners. The horses would pull us through the snow, leaving deep tracks behind us as we made our way to the river, where old Brother and Sister Opstal lived. I could never understand their broken English, and when I gave Mrs. Opstal Grandma's raisin pie, I wondered why she cried.

All these things occurred many years ago, but the memory of

being together as a family for Christmas burns as brightly in my mind today as the flames in the fireplace that kept us warm.

I have a little pillow that hangs from our fireplace all year long. The message reads, in cross-stitch, "All Hearts Return Home for Christmas." The quiet yearning to be home for Christmas does not diminish after childhood or after marriage. Since my husband's parents were not living, it seemed essential that we travel from Utah to Glenwood, Alberta, Canada, every Christmas. It didn't really matter that our car was old and the tires were smooth, that there was no money in our pockets, that the tuna fish sandwiches became very soggy by the second day, and that the radio announced that due to hazardous road conditions people should not travel except in emergencies. There was no question in my mind that being home for Christmas was an emergency.

Over the years we learned that a benevolent and loving Father in Heaven must have appointed angels to be round about us and over us as we traveled the treacherous highways that would take us home. One night, off the road in freezing temperatures and a life-threatening blizzard that made visibility impossible, we waited long enough to be very cold and to realize our total dependence on the Lord. After fervent prayers, in the distance the lights from a big truck approached us. The driver rolled down his window and shouted through the storm, his words revealing his disgust that we were out on a night like that; he even complained about his own foolishness for being on the highway. I'm sure he didn't recognize himself as an angel sent from heaven in answer to our urgent plea for safety, despite what may have been poor judgment on our part. But he was an answer to prayer, and he provided critical help in our time of critical need. Still, whether it was poor judgment or not, we had to respond to the urgency we felt about being home for Christmas. Each year, as long as my parents lived in Canada, we went home for Christmas. Finally, eventually, I learned that you can be home for Christmas in Utah even though Christmases aren't always white there.

The little pillow still hangs on my fireplace with the message, "All Hearts Return Home for Christmas." When our hearts are right we can be home for Christmas every day.

4

A GIFT FOR GRANDMA

I had no idea and could never have imagined things would turn out the way they did. I did not know and could not understand the value of Grandma's black slippers. They were old. They were well worn. They had been the covering for Grandma's feet for as long as I could remember, and Grandma lived with us for several years.

Sitting on the highly polished hardwood floor next to the big rocker in the family room, I would never get tired of listening to Grandma's soft voice as she read to me from the very large book *Hurlbut's Story of the Bible*. Just the way she would hold the book, how she would slow down in some parts of the story and then pick up the speed again, and the expression in the tone of her voice told my young mind that she believed every word she was reading and wanted me to believe also.

She was a real grandma, I thought. Kind of big around the middle that made for good hugging when she would wrap her arms around me and hold me close. She wore her long grey hair in a tidy bun on the top of her head and her glasses down on her nose. As I recall, when she wasn't doing household chores like quietly dusting in the living room during the time the cowboy story about Matt Dillon was playing on the old standup radio, she was in the kitchen stirring up some favorite treat that would fill the room with a wonderful aroma escaping from the oven of the old coal stove. She always wore an apron tied around her waist. Oh, yes, she had a pair of shoes she would wear on Sunday—but as soon as she returned from church the slippers were back on her feet.

A careful study of those black slippers captured my attention. As her voice became more intense when a part of the story seemed particularly important, she would alternately cross one foot over the other.

As we came to the end of our story time one day, I decided to ask Grandma something I had been curious about for some time. Why did her big toes on both feet bulge out at the side, and why were there so many tiny holes in the shoes—like nail punches—that made the bulge look even bigger? Were the holes for decoration or something special? Grandma closed the book, leaned over in the rocker, stretching her legs out and raising both feet up for closer inspection, and began to tell me all about bunions. She explained that it is a swelling around the joint of the big toes, and the little holes that she put in her slippers were not for decoration but rather to relieve the pressure and make it more comfortable to walk. Since Grandma did a lot of walking, that made sense to me. With the mystery solved, I don't remember giving any further thought to Grandma's slippers for quite some time. Except for when she would make some passing comment about needing to replace her slippers, if she only knew where she could find another pair just like them.

It was around the middle of December. The snow was deep. Our mom had a small-town country store right next to our home, and, while she was always close, it was Grandma who kept watch over the house, especially at the time of the "Christmas rush." With so many looking for just the right gift for someone special, Mom was busy in the store. The Christmas tree stood in front of the big window in the living room as our increasing anticipation for Christmas coincided with the lowering of the temperature in the cold Canadian winter. We needed at least a week or two before Christmas to get the tree completely decorated with long shiny silver icicles; they were placed carefully on the branches of the tree one by one. Grandma had helped us make strings of pop-corn and colorful chains out of paper to decorate the tree. We had searched the Eaton's catalogue for our imaginary Christmas wish list, and Grandma couldn't find anything that even resembled her slippers

One bitter cold day, returning home from school around 4:00 P.M., I rushed into the kitchen, knowing Grandma would be there. The room was warm, with heat coming up through the furnace grate in the floor. Dad had stoked the furnace in the basement in anticipation of the lowering temperature. The room was cozy with the added heat from the coal stove in the kitchen. It always seemed warmer when Grandma was there to give a warm hug. I loved my grandma. I had been trying to think of a special present from me to her that she could open Christmas morning and know how much I loved her. Nothing I could think of seemed special enough, even if I had had the money to buy it.

It was right after supper one evening when Grandma announced with firmness, "Now is the time."

"Oh, no," I thought. I absolutely could not believe my eyes. Was this really happening? She walked directly to the coal stove, bent over, and removed her slippers one at a time. She picked up the removable handle, lifted the front plate from the stove, expos-ing the low-burning coals with flames that I could see because I was standing right beside her. She shoved in first one slipper and then the other, replaced the lid, turned immediately, and without hesitation or even a word headed down the hall to her bedroom. I wondered if she was going to shed a few tears in private or get her uncomfortable Sunday shoes. In that split second an idea flashed into my mind. I picked up the handle she had used, removed the plate, and using both hands I grabbed both slippers at once. I removed them from the red-hot coals and beat them against the oven door. A close examination revealed no signs that the fire had damaged those precious slippers and ended their service forever. The discomfort of my hands was of little concern given the plan that had flashed through my mind.

With the slippers hidden behind my back, I walked down the hall to my bedroom and placed my rescued prize in a secret place. I had a plan for my special Christmas gift for Grandma. I shared my excitement with my brother and two sisters and mom and dad with a promise of strictest confidence. The following day Mom helped me find the perfect size box I needed to carry out my plan. I chose the most beautiful Christmas wrapping paper from our store. The wide ribbon I selected from the rack of Christmas wrappings was a bit expensive, Mom said, but she let me have enough to wrap around the box both ways and still have a large, colorful, bright red shiny bow on the top. I attached a brief note that simply said, "Grandma, I love you. I would do anything for you. Merry Christmas. Love, Ardeth." I didn't put the gift under the tree until Christmas Eve. I could hardly wait for Christmas morning, three long days away. I tried to imagine what Grandma would say or do or feel when she opened her gift from me. I hoped it would be the very first gift opened that morning.

For the next two days Grandma's lament about the discomfort of her feet only added to my excitement. Nothing was as comfortable as her old slippers, she repeated more than once. Sitting on the floor by the rocker in the evening while Grandma was reading to me, something was missing—her slippers were not there, just her stockings. She opened the *Hurlbut's Story of the Bible*, going back to re-read the appropriate story for this time of year. The book had beautiful colored pictures. On one side of the open page was the picture labeled "The Nativity," and the other side the picture was labeled "Presentation in the Temple." We studied the pictures in detail before Grandma began to read in her low, soft voice.

"On that night some shepherds were tending their sheep in a field near Bethlehem. Suddenly a light shone upon them, and they saw an angel of the Lord standing before them. They were filled with fear, as they saw how glorious the angel was. But the angel said to them: 'Be not afraid; for behold, I bring you news of great joy, which shall be to all the people; for there is born to you this day in Bethlehem, the city of David, a Savior who is Christ the Lord, the anointed king.'

"Then as quickly as they could go to Bethlehem, they went, and found Joseph, the carpenter of Nazareth, and his young wife Mary and the little baby lying in the manger" (Jesse Lyman Hurlbut, *Hurlbut's Story of the Bible for Young and Old* [New York: Holt, Rinehart, & Winston, 1963], 438). Grandma stopped reading from the book to share feelings from her heart. She seemed anxious for me to connect all the excitement of Christmas with the real story of that first Christmas.

Early Christmas morning, our family was gathered in anticipation around our beautiful Christmas tree. I knew from years past that the time for opening gifts was not yet. On bended knees we would hear Dad's long, long prayer of thanksgiving, and the mention of ever so many who needed special blessings, and gratitude for every family member, his love for the Savior, for food and shelter, and on and on.

The moment of anticipation had finally arrived. Grandma, never putting herself first, sat back, anxious to observe everyone else's excitement. It was agreed that Grandma should be first to open a gift. She pointed to the box with the big red bow that had her name on it. I tried to wait patiently while she removed the ribbon, then slowly loosened the paper from both ends of the package, careful not to tear it so it might be folded and used again and again. Grandma, I thought, does it have to take so long to open your present? I would have removed the ribbon and torn that paper off in a second. The box sat unopened on her lap as she waited ceremoniously to remove the lid. The lid was raised enough for her to peek in. She looked puzzled for only a split second, removed the lid, exposing the contents, and exploded.

"My slippers, my precious slippers!" she exclaimed. She grabbed them from the box, holding them against her chest as she gave me a big hug. "But I put them in the stove!" she exclaimed in wonderment. "They look just the way they were. How can that be? This is like the resurrection," she laughed.

"No, Grandma," I responded. "In the resurrection there will be no bunions."

"Now tell me," she insisted, "how did this happen? I put them in the stove. The fire was burning. I closed the lid and went to my bedroom—then what happened?" Looking straight at me with a big smile, she asked, "How did you retrieve my precious slippers from the fire?"

The family was enjoying every minute of this exciting drama. "Well, Grandma," I began, "you see, I had no money to get you something special that I knew you would really like. What could be better than your old slippers—and they didn't cost me a penny."

Grandma sat beside me, returning the slippers to their rightful place on her feet. I especially liked the look of the bunions on her happy, comfortable feet. Those old slippers remained a part of her daily attire for as long as I can remember.

Now, as Christmas approaches many years later, I look at Grandma's picture and remember. Often the most precious gifts may not cost money, may not come from a store, may not be listed in the Christmas catalogues. The most priceless gifts come from letting family members know just how much you care and that you would go to any length, if possible, to fulfill their wishes.

Now that I am older, with signs of bunions on my own big toes, I can more fully appreciate Grandma's excitement over the recovery of her old black slippers with the tiny holes in the toes. But I also realize more fully that the joy we all felt that Christmas morning was sharing in a little plan that brought us all together in love, excitement, and appreciation in the true spirit of the season.

A TREASURED
CHRISTMAS

The late harvest that year was followed by an early frost, and many of the crops were under a blanket of snow.

As Christmas approached, we children played the wishing game in the Eaton's catalog until the toy section was well marked by the curled edges of the pages. We tried hard to limit our long list of wants to a few special items, knowing that we must be selective since Mom and Dad had to pay Santa for his Christmas treasures. But after a family council to consider a serious matter, our choices were easily made.

Brian, our twelve-year-old crippled cousin who had just been ordained a deacon, was more anxious than ever to walk, and if enough money could be raised, it was possible that the Mayo Clinic in Minnesota could help him. This would require a great sacrifice, but the choice was ours. We could each make our own decision and, if we chose, we could request that the money for our Christmas be given to Brian in hopes of providing medical attention that would allow him to abandon the wheelchair we had all taken turns pushing so often. The Eaton's catalog got lost somewhere in the shuffle as we each talked with great anticipation of our part in helping Brian.

Christmas Eve came, and with it the children's party at the church. I remember being a little disappointed that Santa wore his shabby old suit to our party, but Mom explained that he kept his good one to wear when he came later that night to make his official visit, and that seemed like a good idea to me.

Christmas Eve found cousins, aunts, and uncles all at Mamma Leavitt's big two-story house (she was such a special grandmother that we all called her Mamma Leavitt), and there in her home twenty-one children were tucked into beds of some sort—after hanging up twenty-one stockings. Even as a child, I remember that the air was filled with gaiety, and smiles radiated from the faces of young and old.

The next morning our socks were bulging with goodies. Old dolls had beautiful new wardrobes that Santa had skillfully prepared, and old toys had new paint—and Brian was going to the Mayo Clinic.

It didn't take long to tidy things up since there were very few wrappings, but that was good, because we had exciting things planned with our fathers while our mothers were busy getting ready for the big dinner. The second best turkey in Dad's flock was roasting in the oven and filling the air with that Christmas dinner smell, while the very finest turkey had been selected to go into a big box along with homemade pies, jams, jellies, fruits, and vegetables. On top was a handmade apron carefully wrapped in a piece of soft white tissue paper and tied with a bit of ribbon that had served that same purpose many times before.

Each of us was lifted, all bundled up, onto the big wagon along with the box of goodies, and away we went through the deep snow, listening to the steady rhythm of the horses' hooves until we reached the river about three miles away, where Mr. and Mrs. Opstal lived in their little log house.

The Opstals were an elderly couple from Belgium who had once been wealthy but who had sold all their earthly possessions to flee to freedom in Canada. As we jumped off the wagon into the crunchy snow, we each waited eagerly to be given one of the items from the big box. My brother got to carry the turkey, and I carried one of Mamma Leavitt's delicious raisin pies. It was quite a job trudging through the deep snow, trying to follow in Dad's big steps with our arms loaded.

Inside the one-room home, the bare floors were warmed by a glowing fire, and the long slab table in the middle of the room was gradually piled higher and higher as we each presented our expression of love.

The Opstals couldn't speak a word of English, but I remember thinking that I knew exactly what they were telling us. The words didn't really seem to make any difference, but I was puzzled by their tears when they seemed so happy, and I recall Mom trying to explain this to me later. It didn't make much sense, but as long as they were happy, I guessed it was okay if they wanted to cry.

I'll never forget sitting down to our big dinner with a special place for everyone, including Brian in his wheelchair at the corner of the table because it seemed to fit better there. And down at the far end Papa Leavitt bowed his head and gave a prayer that lasted ever so long.

That night we all got to stay up late, and we sat around the big living room with our moms and dads and talked about things. After our family prayer, when I was tucked into bed, indelibly imprinted on my mind was the lesson that Christmas is an excited, good feeling inside, and how I wished every Christmas might be like this one!

6

SPECIAL GIFTS

It was Christmas Eve. The magic of Christmas seemed more real this year, not so much because of the lights and tinsel but because the feeling of excitement radiated from the inside out. Family members had gathered at our house. After our traditional family dinner, Grandpa gathered us in the living room, where he opened the Bible and read once again the Christmas story from Luke.

"And it came to pass in those days, that there went out a decree from Caesar Augustus" (Luke 2:1), and the story continued. I noticed his hands trembling as he held the sacred record. Grandpa's voice was weaker now, but strong in the message that he and Grandma knew in their hearts and had taught us through the years. After the stockings were finally hung and treats left for

Santa, the children reluctantly, yet eagerly, doubled up in beds, trying hard to get to sleep while listening intensely for any sounds from the expected night visitor. Finally, one by one, each family member had slipped off to bed. The fire was burning low. Now if my husband, Heber, would just go to bed, I could finish my gift for him. I needed about three more hours to complete the plan I had been so excited about and working on for months. But in spite of my encouragement for him to leave, he lingered. It was evident he would wait for me. I decided to go to bed and wait until he dropped off to sleep, then slip out and finish my project for him.

With the lights out and the house quiet, I lay in bed looking into the dark. I was too excited to sleep. I waited to hear his heavy breathing announcing that it would be safe to slip away. To my amazement, and after only a little time, he whispered, "Ardie?" I didn't respond. A conversation now would only delay the time before I could finish my work. When I didn't answer, he slipped out of bed as cautiously as I had planned to. What was he up to? I would go to sleep, I decided. If I could sleep now and awaken about 3:00 A.M. I could still finish my project before six o'clock in the morning, the time Grandpa Ted had agreed we should all gather around the tree.

I woke up off and on during the short night, glanced at the lighted clock, saw that Heber was still not in bed, and tried again to doze off. But I didn't want to fall too soundly asleep and spoil the plan I had been working on so diligently.

Finally, I again woke up, and this time I realized Heber was getting into bed ever so quietly. It was only minutes until his heavy breathing assured me that he was sound asleep. It was 3:00 A.M. If all went well, I could still complete his special gift on time. I knew he would be pleased. "But what in the world kept him up half the night?" I wondered. In just a few hours, I would know; but for now I must concentrate and work fast.

Months earlier we had talked about the forthcoming Christmas and made the traditional gift list that ranged from the ridiculous to the sublime. At the top of my list was a wish that we could have more time together for him to teach me of his great understanding of the gospel. But I was driving two hours each day to BYU, and his schedule was very busy. Our time together was precious.

Heber's list of wants was short, as usual; but he did express a concern for the responsibility he had as a stake president to lead the way, and it bothered him that his family history was not compiled. His family group sheets were incomplete. While the information was probably available from aunts and uncles, his own brothers and sisters had little or no information. He felt anxious about this but wasn't sure it was a Christmas list item, at least not the kind you could get from the mail-order catalog or even ZCMI. That was months earlier, and now my prayer was being answered. The hands on my watch seemed to stand still while I worked. Everything was coming together so beautifully.

The gift was finally wrapped. I could hardly believe I had done it, but there it was—the evidence of hours and hours of work. I hurried back and slipped into bed. It was 5:45 A.M. I had made it! It didn't matter now, and it's a good thing, because children's voices were heard from the other room. "Grandpa says it's time we can get up. Hurry, hurry! We can't wait!" they said. And neither could I. There were so many gifts for everyone.

Heber handed me a package. What in the world could it be? I opened it. It was a box of cassette tapes. On the top of the box was a message: "My dear Ardie. While you are traveling each day, I will be with you and will teach you. As you know, the Doctrine and Covenants has been of special interest to me over the years. I have enjoyed reading and recording for you the entire book. Reading it with the purpose of sharing it with you, I have endeavored to express my interpretation and feelings so that you might feel what I feel about this sacred book. I finished it only a few hours ago. It has been a most rewarding experience for me. Remember the Lord's promise, 'Therefore, if you will ask of me you shall receive; if you will knock it shall be opened unto you.

Now, as you have asked, behold, I say unto you, keep my commandments, and seek to bring forth and establish the cause of Zion; seek not for riches but for wisdom, and behold, the mysteries of God shall be unfolded unto you, and then shall you be made rich. Behold, he that hath eternal life is rich' (D&C 6:5–7). May these tapes add to your wisdom and help unfold the mysteries of God and prepare us for our eternal life together."

I immediately thought of a friend who had recently lost her husband from cancer and wondered what price she would pay for such a gift, to be able to hear her husband's voice read the scriptures to her and her children over and over again, even in his absence. What a priceless gift! No wonder some of his meetings had seemed to last longer than usual. How could I ever thank him enough?

I handed Heber my gift. He tore off the wrapping. A book. A book of remembrance—full. Pages and pages with pictures and stories never before recorded, a result of many secret trips to Ogden while he was in his many meetings, interviewing relatives and sorting through records and histories. The first page of the gift began with a letter: "Dear Heber, As I have copied, reviewed, and prepared these sheets and interviewed family members, your ancestors have become very real to me, and I have an increased appreciation and understanding of the greatness and nobility in the man I married. In interviews with those who knew and remembered your parents, I learned that your father always wanted your mother to be with him, in the fields if possible, and even wherever he was in the house. You must have inherited that. Although I never met your father, and your mother only once, when we meet, I know I'll love them and know them better because of this gift I have prepared for you, which really has been a gift for me."

I don't remember any of the other gifts that year, but Heber and I will never forget the spirit of that glorious Christmas celebration.

7

THE FRAME AND THE YARN

The scent of bayberry candles and burning pine boughs filled the air as we listened to the traditional strains of "Silent night! Holy night! All is calm, all is bright." The firelight was reflected in the faces of our immediate family. It was Christmas Eve, and according to our family tradition, each person could open one gift of his choice before going to bed. This year it would be especially difficult to choose since there had been so many secrets among the family, so much whispering, and so many closed doors, along with occasional shouts of "Don't come in!" It seemed that everyone knew something exciting that someone else wanted to know but must not find out before Christmas.

With the spirit of the season in such abundance, each one was suggesting that someone else be the first to open his gift that night. Little Shelly, who had made several trips over to the tree and back again, always looking in the same area, was now jumping up and down with excitement in her long, pink flannel night-gown. Grandma, sharing her anticipation, took things in hand by explaining to everyone that since Shelly was the youngest, it would seem only right that she should open her Christmas Eve gift first.

It was Shelly's seventh Christmas and, with eyes dancing, and in almost uncontrollable excitement, she pleaded, "Oh, no, Grandma, please not me first. Let me say who's first."

Surprised by her obvious lack of concern for the many gifts addressed to her, everyone quickly agreed to do it Shelly's way and was curious to discover whom she would choose to be first. Without any hesitation, she stretched her arm full length, pointed to me, and said, "You be first." Not yet understanding her intent or why I should be chosen first, I moved on my hands and knees closer to the tree, where I could better examine the gifts that I might choose from. Shelly was on her hands and knees at my side as I began the ritual of deciding which gift to open. No longer able to contain the risk of my making the wrong selection, Shelly jumped in front of me, reaching over all the gifts to a little package that had been carefully placed, half hidden by tinsel and a homemade ornament, between two boughs of the tree. To avoid even a moment's delay, she picked up the little package, which was wrapped in soft, white tissue paper; the paper was somewhat wrinkled by what might have been frequent wrappings and unwrappings, further evidenced by the yarn that fit very loosely around the treasure. As if carrying out a well-rehearsed plan, Shelly, using both hands with great dignity, laid the gift on my lap. I reached out to hug the little gift-bearer, but she jumped back to escape any further delay.

"Open it, open it!" she cried. As the yarn fell free from the package, a squeal escaped Shelly's lips, and she covered her mouth, clasping one hand over the other.

Surely it is in giving that we find the true spirit of Christmas, I thought, as Shelly knelt again at my side. While my intent was to carefully open the precious gift by giving proper respect even to the wrapping, the excited little donor could not endure the waiting. Jumping forth and using both hands, she tore away the paper that had kept her secret too long, holding the prize so close to my face that I was unable to distinguish it. I leaned back to better discern the gift before my eyes.

"I made it for you," she explained. "I made it all myself." Then, letting go of all that she had kept private for what must have seemed forever, she continued to expound on what had been her secret. "I got this frame with these nails around the edge, and then I got this yarn, and I wrapped it a special way." And finally, like a little eruption, she announced, "And it matches! It matches your kitchen!"

With Shelly still holding the precious hot pad, I wrapped her in my arms and wondered what else of any significance could possibly be under the tree—except, that is, for one particular gift. It seemed as if it was taking Shelly's mother forever to unwrap the present she had chosen. She loosened the ribbon, then stopped, laying both hands across the large package on her lap while she joined in conversation that seemed to me to be causing unnecessary delay. I could feel my racing heartbeat and, with one arm around Shelly, I realized I was now experiencing the excitement of *my* secret that had been a long time in the planning.

It began with an old family heirloom, an oval picture frame that we all wanted but that was given to me. This old frame, with its glass curved outward, would be just the thing to safeguard some precious treasures, I had thought. With careful restoration, it took on an elegance and charm made possible only by age and the family sentiment attached to it. Carefully I had cut a piece of canvas the full size of the frame and, using light blue yarn, covered the entire surface with needlepoint. Near the top of the oval the letters L-O-V-E were stitched in a darker blue. In the center I had appliquéd a small portrait of Shelly and her mother in their dark blue nightgowns, sitting together reading bedtime stories. A little pink ballet slipper, with the toe worn completely through by the spirited dancing of a three-year-old, also became a part of the collection, more treasured now than when it was new. A piece of Shelly's light blue Alice in Wonderland costume, made originally for Halloween, then used as her official dancing gown, and now worn and torn, had been rescued, along with a bit of tattered eyelet, and placed among the treasures. Conspicuously near the center was a shiny blonde curl, tied with a bit of light blue yarn, from Shelly's first haircut.

Although the wrapping had not yet disclosed my prize, the minute detail of this gift was vivid in my mind. Uncontrollably, I reached out with one hand to assist Shelly's mom, exposing my reason for excitement. As she saw the gift and considered the full meaning of my offering, I began explaining. "I made it for you," I said. "You see, I took this frame, and then I got some yarn, and . . ."

Something about the sound of the words "the frame" and "the yarn" echoed like a rehearsal from Shelly's performance telling about her gift to me. Through my own replay of this little experience came new insight, increased awareness, and a sensitivity to a teaching moment that had been staged by Shelly.

Oblivious for a few moments to the events around me, I

pondered the meaning of this incident. Who was the teacher? Was she also the student? Was there only one who learned, or did each contribute to the teaching? Was anyone left out of the learning? Is not a teaching moment meant for all?

Two frames, some yarn, and the accumulation of other precious items became the objects for our celebration of love and affection at this joyous Christmas season. The result of thoughtful advance planning—providing gifts from the heart—was equally enjoyed by the giver and the receiver. Gifts that continue to increase in value are those given through a labor of love, heartfelt and unconditional love, Christlike love.

"Neither was the teacher any better than the learner; and thus they were all equal, and they did all labor, every man according to his strength" (Alma 1:26).

8

ANOTHER KIND OF WHITE CHRISTMAS

Since I grew up in Alberta, Canada, I never had to dream of a white Christmas. There was always plenty of snow and cold at Christmastime. At least that's how I remember it.

In 1992, after many years of Christmas in Utah, Heber and I returned to Canada, where we would be for the next three years. This time we were not in Alberta but in British Columbia, and we were not with our family but with over 450 wonderful missionaries over the course of three years, who indeed became our family.

Through that experience we became awakened to a new and wonderful dimension of the idea of being home for Christmas. A mission would bring the first Christmas away from home for most missionaries, maybe all of them. It would be quite a different experience from the traditions of family gatherings they were accustomed to. I wondered: Can a branch of a pine tree, tied inartistically with a bit of red ribbon, and a candle on a table in a humble missionary apartment make a Christmas? Would they hang their stockings, and if they did would they fill their own or each other's? What about the lights on the tree they were used to? What about all the good food? Could they experience a real Christmas away from all the family traditions that seem to make it real?

Our mission covered a very large area, some of it accessible only over snowy and treacherous mountain roads. We couldn't bring the missionaries all together, but we could go to them and meet in small groups. Could this be like Christmas, I wondered? We began our zone conferences early in the month of December. During each one, after the usual training, we gathered together for a Christmas program, hoping to create a spirit that in some way would focus on the true meaning of Christmas without fueling the feeling of homesickness that was already obvious in the countenances of some. The program began with a readers' theater. Each one, taking turns, stood and read a part of the Christmas story, first from the Bible and then from the Book of Mormon. Hymns were sung at appropriate intervals, supporting the message being read. In some zones, soloists added greatly to the quality of the performance.

In each small gathering of young elders and sisters, the zone leader addressed the group, speaking with excitement, enthusiasm, and conviction of the plans for a white Christmas. In the northern end of the province, there was no question they would have a white Christmas. They could have a white Christmas on the first of July (Canada Day), it seemed to me. In Vancouver, there wouldn't be snow, but rain for sure. But the zone leader (each of them in turn) was undeterred, insisting it would indeed be a white Christmas. Then he would clarify: "Can you see yourself dressed all in white?" he asked. "Can you see yourself with the investigator you are teaching, praying for, and loving with all of your heart? Can you see him or her also dressed in white, ready to enter the waters of baptism together? Can you feel the joy of Christmas in the greatest gift ever given? Will you strive to bring that gift of eternal life to a brother or sister this year by your diligence and obedience, as you teach with the Spirit and testify of what you know to be true?"

As each of these young leaders stood before his group and spoke of a "white" Christmas in his own way, the message was clear. "This is the season when we commemorate Christ's birth, His mission, His life, His love, and His atonement," one elder explained. "'For behold, the field is white, all ready to harvest,' and we *can* have a white Christmas," he insisted. They didn't talk of turkey and trimmings; they spoke of fasting and prayer. They didn't speak of packages to be unwrapped, but of gifts of the Spirit. They didn't speak of spending but of saving—saving souls.

In the beautiful city of Vancouver, about twenty of the foreign-language-speaking missionaries stood on a platform in the center of the large mall and sang songs about that holy night. These young men, in white shirts and dark suits, sang to the passersby in their own languages, first in Mandarin, then Cantonese, then Vietnamese, and Spanish. People stopped, listened, felt something inside, and wondered and lingered. It was easy to step up and simply say, "Would you like to know something about these young men, and why they are here, and the gift they have for you?" Some agreed to have the missionaries come to their homes and bring the "gift": a message of hope, of peace in a troubled world—the message of eternal life, the restoration of the gospel of Jesus Christ for all mankind in every language and every land.

There were many dressed in white who entered the waters of baptism that Christmas season. It was a white Christmas for sure, with nothing missing. Everything that mattered was there and so much, much more. If we were not home for Christmas, surely we felt closer to our ultimate home than ever before. I began to review in my mind the highlights of my childhood memories of

Christmas, and in a magical way it was as though every piece was in place, now magnified by years of experience.

I met a Chinese couple, recent converts, who took me in memory to dear old Brother and Sister Opstal of Alberta. I couldn't understand their broken English, but the gift the missionaries gave them of the gospel of Jesus Christ filled their eyes with tears of joy and gratitude. I understood better now why there were tears in Sister Opstal's eyes when I gave her Grandma's raisin pie so many years before.

We didn't have musical accompaniment except for the piano—no family orchestra or grandpa to lead the music—but the Spirit was surely present at each zone conference as the missionaries stood and sang the songs of Christmas. They always ended with "Silent night! Holy night! All is calm, all is bright," which seemed to open a conduit between heaven and earth. They didn't sound like the Tabernacle Choir, and they couldn't sing the "Hallelujah Chorus," but as I listened, not with my ears but with the Spirit that was present, I wanted to stand and shout "Hallelujah!" with an increasing sense of the true meaning of Christmas.

There were few, if any, of the traditional Christmas lights to adorn the humble apartments of these young missionaries, but the traditional Christmas lights would be paled by the light that shone in the eyes of the missionaries and the newly baptized members as they came forth from the waters of baptism. It was a light penetrating the darkness of the world not just at Christmastime, but all year long.

One Chinese brother, a convert, had lost his wife through cancer just before Christmas. Funerals are hard at any time, but certainly they are harder still at Christmastime. I stood and looked at the coffin so beautifully lined with white satin, and the memories of my childhood Christmas played across my mind. Now the thoughts of death brought to mind the message of eternal life and the deeper understanding of the Christmas story: Christ's life, His mission, His death, His resurrection, and how the meaning of the Atonement takes away the fear of death, especially at Christmastime. It was explained to the children that their mother had returned home, home to our Heavenly Father. She would be home for Christmas.

The missionaries received boxes of socks and ties and broken cookies, but their list of wants this year could not be purchased with money.

At the close of each day, with our energy spent, we found ourselves on our knees in lengthy prayer as we pleaded for our little band of stripling warriors in the great army for Christ, both as a group and individually. Looking back now, I see that Grandpa's prayers were not as lengthy as I had remembered them being.

The days were marked off on the calendar as Christmas came and passed. We waited anxiously for the letters the missionaries wrote each week, reporting on their highs, their lows, their successes, their discouragements, their challenges, and their victories. After many weeks it became quite easy to detect in the first sentence or two the success or struggle that contributed to the "growth experience" that week. Then the letters following Christmas began to arrive, and with few exceptions the same messages were repeated over and over: "My best Christmas so far." "I've never had such a feeling of love as I've had this year." "It never gets better than this." "This was a real Christmas." These young men and women celebrated the birth of Christ as they represented Him and testified of Him, as they invited others to follow Him. They knocked on doors and exclaimed, "We have come with a message from Jesus Christ about His birth. May we come in?" With this simple and sincere approach, they did enter into the homes, the hearts, and the lives of many. They taught of home, our ultimate home, and our family relationship.

Another year came and went. It was one week before Christmas in the second year of our mission. New missionaries were arriving and others were returning home, having completed their missions. Something wonderful and magnificent happens for missionaries between the time they arrive in the mission field and that day (which initially seems so far away) when they return home. Their experience is paralleled in the story of the wise men. Let me explain.

Matthew gives the account of the wise men going in search of Jesus. They found Him and offered Him their gifts of gold, frankincense, and myrrh. "And being warned of God in a dream that they should not return to Herod, they departed into their own country another way" (see Matthew 2:11–12). While Matthew says correctly that they took another route to avoid King Herod, there is a more significant message in this account. The wise men, having found the Savior, went home "another way." Having found the Christ Child, they were never the same again; they could not go back to their old ways.

During a mission, during the days and weeks of tracting and teaching and struggling and growing and testifying of Jesus Christ; through the experience of being filled with the power of the message confirmed by the Holy Ghost, even when it seemed stormy outside; through the experience of being off the highway in a snowbank, with the passersby shouting words of disgust and abuse—through all this, yet the missionaries found Him. It was not as a babe in a manger, as the wise men found, but they found

Him and we heard them testify, "He is my Lord, my Savior, my Redeemer, my God." They found Him and were ready to return home "another way," filled with a witness of the Spirit they could not deny. They came as young men and women, became true disciples of the Lord Jesus Christ through their missionary experiences, and would return home another way.

"Will there ever be another Christmas like this one?" questioned one, bearing testimony of the power of the Spirit he had come to know.

The answer is yes—if we continue to follow the Lord's way. President Howard W. Hunter told us how, with these impelling words: "We must know Christ better than we know him; we must remember him more often than we remember him; we must serve him more valiantly than we serve him" (in Conference Report, April 1994, 84).

It is in the mission field that we all come to know Him better, remember Him more often, and serve Him every day, sharing His message not just at Christmastime but all year long. If we will do that, not only as missionaries, but as their "fellow servants," we will find Him in our hearts and in our homes and in our lives. If we will bring our gifts—not of gold, frankincense, and myrrh, but of service, sacrifice, love, testimony, and good will—we will find Him and go home another way.

THE LITTLE
LAMB

When our Christmas tree is dismantled and all the other decorations, including the olive wood and porcelain Nativity pieces, are tucked away in their boxes for yet another year, a little wooden lamb with a face covered in black and gray yarn is returned to its place, front and center, in the china closet near the main entrance of our home. This gift is never tucked away. It remains in its place through every season, except at Christmastime when it is placed with the other animals near the small figures representing Joseph, Mary, and the Babe in the manger.

A little woolly lamb among the delicate pieces in a china closet? one might ask. Yes, a lamb far more precious than china. Not because of its sale value, of course, but because of its symbolic *soul* value.

It stands as a constant reminder of a soul—a black sheep, so to speak—and the price paid for its rescue. Symbolically, a black sheep is one who has wandered from the path and is not with the ninety and nine safely within the fold. It is dependent upon the shepherd—the Good Shepherd—for rescue.

In the parable of the lost sheep, Jesus asks: "What man of you, having an hundred sheep, if he lose one of them, doth not leave the ninety and nine in the wilderness, and go after that which is lost, until he find it? And when he hath found it, he layeth it on his shoulders, rejoicing. And when he cometh home, he calleth together his friends and neighbours, saying unto them, Rejoice with me; for I have found my sheep which was lost" (Luke 15:4–6).

Whether we have wandered from the path or not, are we not all dependent on the Good Shepherd for His love, His mercy, and His atoning sacrifice? This message is captured in the words of the song by Henry W. Baker:

> *The King of love my Shepherd is,*
> *Whose goodness faileth never;*
> *I nothing lack if I am His*
> *And He is mine forever: . . .*
> *Perverse and foolish oft I strayed,*

But yet in love He sought me,
And on His shoulder gently laid,
And home, rejoicing, brought me.

This little lamb, which has become a symbol for remembering, arrived in the mail following a women's conference I attended in a distant location. I had been asked to speak on the worth of a soul and faith in the Lord Jesus Christ. Just before the meeting began, I learned that, while we all need reassurance of our worth, there was a sister who hopefully would be in the audience who was struggling desperately with a devastating problem of addiction. She had lost her feeling of worth, of her infinite worth. She seldom attended church, perhaps not feeling worthy or accepted. She had wandered from the path—a black sheep, one might say.

The sorrowful circumstance of this sister was known to very few. Even her family members, except for one or two, were not aware of the burden she was carrying. I did not know and could not identify in the audience of approximately 350 sisters which one was carrying this heavy load. Who is this lost sheep who has wandered temporarily from the path? I wondered. The wanderers are often not easily identified by the natural eye and may be overlooked by those who might help if they were aware. Although we as members of His Church have covenanted to carry one another's burdens, we are often oblivious to the weight another carries. From all outward appearances, everyone seemed included safely within the fold. I wondered what I might say to this sister, whichever one she was, that might lift her burden while others listened in.

The message of the Good Shepherd brings rest to the weary, hope for the discouraged, and a promise that through faith in the atonement of Jesus Christ and repentance of our sins we can receive strength and assistance to do what we cannot do if left to our own means. This grace, an enabling power, makes it possible to gain eternal life and exaltation after we expend our best efforts (see LDS Bible Dictionary, "Grace," 697). With concern for this dear sister, I emphasized that this enabling power does not come at the end of our lives when we've done the best we can, but that it is a daily, hourly source of strength through the grace of God.

Continuing to search the audience for "the one," I turned to the words of Mormon, which give reason for hope: "Behold I say unto you that ye shall have hope through the atonement of Christ and the power of his resurrection, to be raised unto life eternal, and this because of your faith in him according to the promise" (Moroni 7:41).

In the audience, a few rows back and off to the side, was a sister I had noticed slipping onto the end of a bench a few minutes late. She did not look up but sat with her head bowed. At one point, I observed, she was wiping her eyes. Could this be the sister in the flock who needs the reassurance that the Good Shepherd is concerned for the one? I wondered.

As I spoke, my gaze returned again and again to this sister until our eyes met. At that moment it seemed the message of the conference might be for her and her alone—the one. Now, without looking in her direction, I turned to the Doctrine and Covenants to share the Savior's encouraging words: "Behold, ye are little children and ye cannot bear all things now; ye must grow in grace and in the knowledge of the truth. Fear not, little children, for you are mine, and I have overcome the world, and you are of them that my Father hath given me; and none of them that my Father hath given me shall be lost" (D&C 50:40–42).

Once again our eyes met. The words of President Joseph F. Smith came to my mind: "God does not judge men as we do, nor look upon them in the same light that we do. He knows our imperfections—all the causes, the 'whys and wherefores' are made manifest unto Him. He judges us by our acts and the intents of our hearts. His judgments will be true, just and righteous; ours are obscured by the imperfections of man" (in *Journal of Discourses* [London: Latter-day Saints' Book Depot, 1854–86], 24:78).

Following the meeting, this sister I had been especially drawn to stood apart from the others until only a few remained. She must have known I had felt the Spirit touch her heart. She stepped forward and said only a word, then slipped a note into my hand and quickly walked away. The brief note revealed what I had supposed. She was the lamb, or perhaps one of the lambs, who hungered for the assurance of the worth of a soul, her soul. She had felt the Savior's love.

One week following the conference, I received a letter postmarked in the city where the conference had been held. I opened the letter and began reading a message I share in part:

"I want to thank you for the special gift of hope. Since that Saturday night I have been so filled with the Spirit, I have walked around for days now with a lump in my throat. For the first time in years I have prayed to my Father in Heaven and feel hope. I'm longing to come 'home.' I feel such an urgency to change. How appropriate at this time of year. I've always felt like the last leaf on the tree, clinging for all it's worth, not courageous enough to let go and fall, afraid the fall will hurt. I hang on all alone. I wish I could find words to thank you for the message of hope.

"This fall as I watch the golden leaves break loose and drift from their branches, I will give thanks. Maybe someone else has regained their testimony also and found courage to let go because a hand was there to hold."

This dear sister would learn that His hand is always there to hold. He is the Good Shepherd. We are the lambs of His fold, and He will encircle us in the arms of His love (see D&C 6:20).

> *Dear to the heart of the Shepherd,*
> *Dear are the lambs of his fold;*
> *Some from the pastures are straying,*
> *Hungry and helpless and cold.*
> *See, the Good Shepherd is seeking,*
> *Seeking the lambs that are lost,*
> *Bringing them in with rejoicing,*
> *Saved at such infinite cost.*
> *Out in the desert they wander,*
> *Hungry and helpless and cold;*
> *Off to the rescue he hastens,*
> *Bringing them back to the fold.*
>
> (*Hymns*, no. 221)

I did not anticipate as Christmas approached that year what a priceless gift I would receive. Among the letters and cards from friends far and wide came a small package carrying the return address of the sister who had written to me following the women's conference. I opened the package, unfolded the soft white tissue paper, and held in my hands a little wooden lamb, with a face covered in black and gray yarn, and a brief note: "Please don't forget me. I'm the black sheep."

While we return in celebration and tradition to the birth of the Babe in the manger each Christmas, is it possible that we could ever overlook the purpose of His life, His atonement, His resurrection, and His great gift of eternal life for each of us, when we know that He will never forget us, never leave us, that He will stand by us? He is our advocate with the Father. He is our Savior, our Redeemer, and our Friend.

It is the little black lamb in my china closet that serves as a reminder all year long of the greatest gift ever given. He came to save saints and sinners and all in between. His purpose is clearly stated: "For behold, this is my work and my glory—to bring to pass the immortality and eternal life of man" (Moses 1:39). He is the Good Shepherd; we are the sheep.

President Gordon B. Hinckley explained: "We honor the birth of our Lord, the Son of God, who condescended to come to earth because He loved us. He came to do for us that which we could not do for ourselves. Without His Atonement we would be helpless before the unrelenting grasp of death. Our destiny would be that dark and dismal 'country from whose bourn no traveler returns.' We would stand hopeless and helpless in our sins, going nowhere, making no progress.

"But because of Him—and Him alone—there is hope, there is peace, there is light and understanding. Through His great act of redemption, through His atoning sacrifice, came eternal life. The gift of the resurrection is afforded all, and the opportunity for eternal progress and eventual exaltation is granted those who will listen to Him and obey Him" (*Discourses of President Gordon B. Hinckley, 1995–1999* [Salt Lake City: Deseret Book, 2005], 410–11).

The little lamb, a gift from one giving thanks for hope and asking never to be forgotten, is never put away.

In the book of Isaiah, we read: "Come now, and let us reason together, saith the Lord: though your sins be as scarlet, they shall be as white as snow; though they be red like crimson, they shall be as wool" (Isaiah 1:18). Close to the little black woolly lamb in my china closet is another lamb—this one with wool as white as snow. Between the two stands a small porcelain figure of the Savior, not as a babe in the manger, but as our Savior with arms outstretched.

And His message is clear: "Behold the wounds which pierced my side, and also the prints of the nails in my hands and feet; be faithful, keep my commandments, and ye shall inherit the kingdom of heaven" (D&C 6:37).

He was the Lamb of God, perfect and without blemish. The gift He bought with a dear price is the greatest of all gifts, that of eternal life. May we "always remember him and keep his commandments . . . that [we] may always have his Spirit to be with [us]" (D&C 20:77) and feel unbounded gratitude at this Christmas season and always.

"I TOLD YOU HE WOULD KNOW ME"

A few years ago, as Christmas drew near, I found myself confronted with a very full schedule. The streets were crowded, my calendar was crowded, and my mind was crowded. There was so much to do and so little time. An invitation to give a brief Christmas message to the residents of a nursing home nearby was one activity I could check off rather quickly and then move to the next appointment.

As I rushed past the receptionist at the nursing home door, I was ushered into a large room—where I suddenly stopped. Life was moving at a different pace here, if it was moving at all. There were wheelchairs, bent shoulders, gray hair, tired eyes, and the impression of so little going on. Though the room was warm, many of the elderly had knitted shawls draped over rounded shoulders and woolly slippers covering tired feet.

Following my message, one of the visitors, the granddaughter of one of the elderly residents, asked if I had time to visit with her grandmother in her own private room for just a few moments. She commented, "She thinks she knows you," indicating perhaps that her grandmother's mind might also be tired. I agreed that I could spare a few minutes, and I followed the younger woman as she helped her elderly grandmother shuffle down the narrow hall to her room. When she reached her bedside, this dear elderly woman slowly turned around, let go of her granddaughter's arm, and sat on her bed. Then she raised her head so that I could look into her face. My eyes caught hers. "Sister Myrtle Dudley!" I exclaimed. "You were my Primary teacher!"

Her wrinkled mouth formed a smile as she pulled on her granddaughter's jacket and said, "See, I told you she would know me."

I continued: "I remember when you used to lead the singing. You wore that wine-colored dress with the big sleeves that waved back and forth as you taught us the songs."

Again she pulled on her granddaughter's jacket. "I told you she would know me."

"Yes," I said, "and you made carrot juice for my mother when she was sick."

Then she asked, "Did you come all the way from Canada just to see me?"

"Oh, Sister Dudley," I said, "I have come a long way. It has been over forty years."

She reached out her arms and drew me close. I felt like a child once again, back in Primary, in the arms of my teacher who loved me. Then she whispered in my ear, "I knew you would know me."

There in the arms of my Primary teacher the world stood still for a moment. The busy streets were forgotten. The crowded calendar was no longer pressing on my mind. The spirit of Christmas filled my soul. A small miracle was taking place, not because of what I brought but because of what I received.

After a time, I reluctantly left the presence of my Primary teacher and walked slowly back to my car. I sat there pondering while the snowflakes fell gently on the windshield. It was the season of celebration for the birth of Jesus Christ, our Lord and Savior. It was He who asked us to love one another and to serve one another. He said to each of us, "Inasmuch as ye have done it unto one of the least of these my brethren, ye have done it unto me" (Matthew 25:40).

Yes, I thought, I knew Sister Dudley because she had served me, and she knew me because she had served me. Then the vision cleared before my eyes. We will know Him when we serve Him, and He will know us when we serve Him. And I asked myself, Can I one day say with the same confidence with which Sister Dudley spoke, "I told you He would know me"?

Let us always keep in mind an anticipation of that glorious day when we will be with our Father again. The words of President George Q. Cannon help us envision that event: "We existed with Him in the family relationship as His children. . . . When we see our Father in heaven we shall know Him; and the recollection that we were once with Him and that He was our Father will come back to us, and we will fall upon His neck, and He will fall upon us, and we will kiss each other. We will know our Mother, also" (*Gospel Truth* [Salt Lake City: Deseret Book, 1987], 3, 5).

One day we will leave this stage of life. I am confident that, having done our part, we will receive an embrace and experience the greatest commendation we could ever hope for from the only one who really matters. "You played your part so very, very well," I believe we will hear our Father and Mother say. "My child, I have you home again." Then we will hear not with our ears, but with our spirits, the echoing applause of multitudes of heavenly hosts, our brothers and our sisters, rejoicing in our safe return to have glory added upon our heads forever and ever.

11

A CHRISTMAS NEVER TO
BE FORGOTTEN

It was all over except the memories. What we hoped would happen, happened. The year was drawing to a close and a new year was just around the corner. But for years to come this Christmas would never be forgotten—not because of the number of nice gifts or the good food or the fun parties, but because of what we had all experienced. It began during a family home evening near the first of December, when we gathered together, moms and dads, brothers and sisters, aunts and uncles and cousins. We were each invited to share our ideas about what would make this Christmas one to remember. As each one, young and older, made his or her suggestions, the list became rather lengthy. Ideas included the Christmas tree, of course, with all the trimmings that had been used over many years; the Nativity story read and acted out, which we would all participate in by playing a part or by being an appreciative audience; Christmas lights inside and out; all the cooking for a special dinner; our annual talent show, where everyone receives a rousing applause; and on and on. After the suggestions died down and had been recorded for follow up later, there was one more question for everyone to consider.

"Thank you for your good suggestions of all the things we are going to do," I said. "But now let's talk about what we want to have happen." There was a curious look in the eyes of some. I continued: "When we know what we want to have happen we can plan with a purpose. When we are clear about our purpose then the things we do help make it happen." This was a new idea that needed further explanation. One comment reflected the thoughts of others. "What do you mean, 'plan with a purpose'? Doesn't it just happen?"

"Oh, yes," I agreed. "Christmas will come and go—but what if we could think of something that we could plan with a purpose in our mind and then make it happen?"

It takes longer when you plan that way. The ideas did not come quite so quickly, but with patience many thoughts were shared, and we settled on three special experiences we would plan for this Christmas.

First, we tried to think of something that would help us feel close to Grandpa and Grandma. Second, Kent, in the fourth grade, wanted to know what the poor kids do in faraway places. Third, we wanted to feel that we were tied closely together as a family, "so no one would ever be lost." Following that evening our plans began to unfold. It was magical as we attempted to carry out our plans.

PLAN 1. A small, real Christmas tree was carefully selected. While we decorated the little tree, we talked about Christmas at Grandpa and Grandma's when they were alive. The children had many questions as they placed long, thin, silver icicles one by one on the tree about one inch apart, just like Grandma used to. "Did you really ride in a sleigh with horses pulling it when you took Grandma's pies to the family that lived down by the river?" was one of the many questions that invited discussion and many stories, until the tree that was an important part of our plan was completely covered with icicles.

It was just before sundown on Christmas Eve. The temperature outside was cold, but no one wanted to be left behind. We dressed in warm coats and parkas and gloves and mittens and scarves and hats and boots before loading into the cars heading for the cemetery not too far away. Going to the cemetery at Christmastime was a new experience for us. As we trudged through the deep snow, leaving a trail behind, we followed the leader, who was carrying the tree to be placed on Grandpa's and Grandma's grave. Everyone but the children in arms helped clear the deep snow from the headstone. The beautiful little tree was carefully put in its place. It was very quiet as we stood in a circle around Grandpa's and Grandma's grave, with many other headstones in view. There was a sense of reverence as we began to sing. In some magical way a gentle wind began to blow, and the shimmering silver icicles on the tree seemed almost alive.

One of the children asked, "Do you think they know we are here?" We agreed that it felt like it. It felt like Grandpa and Grandma were not that far away and that they remembered us at this Christmas time, as we remembered them. We didn't want to leave. We remained as the sun was setting and took turns suggesting the Christmas songs we would sing next. It seemed like angels accompanied us as the sound of our voices filled the night air singing, "Silent night! Holy night!"

Returning home, we talked about how we felt and how the decorated tree seemed to help connect us with the past and how the gentle wind blew just at the right time. One comment from a cousin—"It was really cool"—brought a quick response from another: "Cool? I thought it was cold." The temperature outside did not penetrate the warm feelings in our hearts. The Spirit told us that Grandpa and Grandma were aware that we were there. It was a special experience we will not forget.

PLAN 2. Following our experience at Grandpa's and Grandma's graveside, we returned to our traditional Christmas Eve dinner with all the trimmings, followed by the reading of the Christmas story from Luke 2, and then a presentation of the Christmas pageant, with everyone taking part as a performer or an appreciative audience.

After putting the food out for Santa and hanging the stockings, before the children were tucked into bed, everyone was permitted, according to tradition, to open just one gift. It was usually hard to decide which one to choose, but this year Kent's curiosity left no question in his mind. Among the many beautifully wrapped presents under the tree were several small gifts, wrapped in old newspaper and tied with twine, that stood apart from all the others. One of those curious gifts had Kent's name on it. When it was his turn, he quickly broke the string and tore the newspaper off. He appeared a bit disappointed to find only a white T-shirt. He held it up for all to see. Across the front was the picture of a father and a young boy driving a water buffalo. Across the back was the name of an African village, Ouelessebougou. There was also a video in the package. A note was enclosed explaining that money had been donated in Kent's name to the

Ouelessebougou–Utah Alliance to help buy a much needed water buffalo for a family in faraway Africa.

After we watched the brief video telling about some children who lived in that faraway place, Kent was anxious to find out: "Did they get a whole buffalo from me?" he asked. I explained that the donation in his name would probably not be enough to buy a whole buffalo, but it would have purchased at least part of one. "How much would it cost to buy a whole buffalo?" he eagerly asked. I told him I didn't know. This thought remained in his young mind all through Christmas. When he returned to school he had a plan. On his own he talked to his friends and began to organize his fourth-grade class in an attempt to raise enough money to buy "a whole water buffalo for the kids in Africa." He was driven by his desire to help. Additional money was donated.

PLAN 3. During the last stages of my father's stomach cancer, he and I used to walk every day a short distance from our home to the construction site of a large bridge that was needed to span Barton Creek. One evening in the twilight, the noise of the construction quieted for the day, Dad and I stood leaning against a big earth-moving tractor at the bridge site. No traffic interrupted our privacy, since there was as yet no bridge for crossing. "Dad," I asked in a teasing tone, "how come you are so anxious about the completion of this bridge?" He smiled and stroked his chin and, without any introduction or explanation, began quoting from his reservoir of memorized poetry.

That was years before. The bridge had been completed for quite some time and crossed over hundreds of times. Remembering my time on the bridge with my dad, I determined the bridge would be the perfect setting for part three of our plan. On Christmas day, when the festivities were over, we all met together on the bridge where Grandpa used to walk. With our arms around each other and the little children snuggling in the arms of a parent or sibling, we stood together. We managed to wrap a very wide, long ribbon around ourselves and tie it in a large knot. We were literally tied together on the bridge. Then I read the poem that Grandpa had memorized and recited near the completion of the bridge and the completion of his life several years before.

> *An old man going a lone highway*
> *Came at the evening, cold and gray,*
> *To a chasm, vast and wide and steep,*
> *With waters rolling cold and deep.*
> *The old man crossed in the twilight dim,*
> *That sullen stream had no fears for him;*
> *But he turned when safe on the other side,*
> *And built a bridge to span the tide.*

"Old man," said a fellow pilgrim near,
"You are wasting your strength with building
here.
Your journey will end with the ending day,
You never again will pass this way.
You've crossed the chasm, deep and wide,
Why build you this bridge at eventide?"

The builder lifted his old gray head.
"Good friend, in the path I have come," he said,
"There followeth after me today
A youth whose feet must pass this way.
This chasm that has been naught to me
To that fair-haired youth may a pitfall be.
He, too, must cross in the twilight dim—
Good friend, I am building the bridge for him."

(Will Allen Dromgoole, "The Bridge Builder")

We stood quietly pondering the real bridge that Grandpa had helped build for us. I believe we each promised in our hearts that we would stay tied together as a family, and when it came time to cross the bridge and follow Grandpa and Grandma, we would still be tied together—children, grandchildren, and great-grandchildren for generations to come. In the circle we talked about how we would help each other and love each other and forgive each other and pray for each other. We felt tied together in a bond much tighter than the ribbon.

Now, years later, we talk about that Christmas when we first planned with a purpose. We can hardly remember any of the gifts we shared that year except for the white T-shirts with the father and son driving a water buffalo on the front. But we all remember that when we took time to decide what we wanted to have happen, we began to plan with a purpose. We wanted to have an experience that would help us feel close to Grandma and Grandpa, and we did. We wanted an experience that would help us feel that we were tied close together as a family forever, and we did. Kent wanted us to have a feeling for poor kids in faraway places, and we did.

Some time after Christmas, when many things were put away and forgotten, we gathered for what you might call an evaluation. Did what we wanted to have happen, happen? It was agreed that planning with a purpose was a great idea. That evening, it was suggested that we plan our summer vacations with a purpose and our birthday parties with a purpose and maybe that should be the beginning of every plan. Now, these many years later, when someone in our family asks the question, "What shall we do?" someone else pipes up with the familiar inquiry, "What do you want to have happen?" Once that is decided, we have come to believe, then it can happen.

When we find ourselves pondering God's eternal plan, we come to know unquestionably that it is a plan with a purpose. We know what it is He wants to have happen. His plan is clear. His purpose is clear. As we prepare ourselves to cross the bridge, may we each do our part to carry out His plan. When we do, we can be sure that what we want to have happen will happen.

ABOUT THE AUTHOR

Ardeth Greene Kapp served as Young Women general president of The Church of Jesus Christ of Latter-day Saints. She later accompanied her husband, Heber, in his assignment as president of the Canada Vancouver Mission and served as matron of the Cardston Alberta Temple, where her husband was the president. She has also served on the boards of several corporations, including Deseret Book, the Deseret News, and Utah Youth Village. Sister Kapp is a popular speaker and bestselling author of more than a dozen books, including *Better Than You Think You Are*.